Remember

Elise Pauly

BookLeaf Publishing

Presentation by *BookLeaf Publishing*

Web: www.bookleafpub.com

E-mail: info@bookleafpub.com

ISBN: 9789357212076

First edition 2023

PREFACE

Thank you for reading this book. I hope that it some way it helps all who read it.

Memories

Some are bright and some dull
Some cause chaos and others lull
Some make confusion and others sense
Some can relax and others make tense

Some may fade over the years
Some may bring many tears
Some one never does forget
Some are of people you've met

People that never leave your mind
People that did leave you behind
In your perilous journey through life
Left when you were enduring strife

Perhaps a saying with no source
Perhaps a tinge of remorse
For one does not remember as well
All the stories that they might tell

But alas we sometimes forget
The things we've seen and the people we've met
But that is alright for me and you
For we make more memories, all brand new

Friend

How to be a good friend
To reassure a heart on the mend
To always stay and never leave
To tell the truth and not deceive

To endure during harder days
To shine like sun rays
A friend reminds you of your worth
That has built up since your birth

Someone to confide every secret to
A friend who sticks right beside you
And makes you better and stronger
Who is there not for a short time but longer

Someone you would lay down your life for
Someone who you love more and more
Someone who shares your laughs and tears
Someone who helps you face your fears

This is what a good friend can be
Who shows you things that you'd never see
Things about yourself that make you great
These all make a really good best mate

Smile

That picture perfect smile
Doesn't last for a while
Those full of hope eyes
Are dulled by the lies

That focus to succeed
With every word and deed
That need to never fail
To be the strongest female

The high expectations to meet
Have one broken down and beat
The need to always do better
Turns everything else into a blur

The focus to be the best
The need to pass every test
Not simply pass but to excel
Not do okay but very well

The nagging need for perfection
The crippling fear of rejection
Tears down the strongest of them all
And builds up a high brick wall

Between them and others around
Between many a negative sound
Hoping that it protects their heart
So that their life won't fall apart

That sweet innocent smile
Never lasts for a while
Those pure loving eyes
Always dim with lies

Warring Eyes

One can see in peoples eyes
Their struggles and their battle cries
How hard they're fighting to survive
How much they long to simply thrive

Each morning some awake in despair
Some awake around people who care
Some wake up with joy for the day
And some on beds continue to lay

Each person has a war to fight
Some with no end in sight
The war begins out of the womb
And ends when one is in a tomb

People fight and people give in
People lose wars and some they win
But each battle begins to drain
And each fight increases the pain

Trying not to give in against it all
Trying to rise each time they fall
One can't see what they'll face
Along this tiring and long race

Yet still people endure to the end
They don't break even when they bend
They try not to let the enemy win
They try not to let the doubts in

Rain

Drops streak down the window
Rain soaking the earth below
Wheels spraying water everywhere
Everyone going about without a care

Rain makes everything look so new
The huge drops make quite the view
As one drives on through the torrent
Missing this perfect natural moment

The water washes everything clean
No smudge or dirt can be seen
The beautiful and perfect display
As nature for a moment has its way

Rain can be a favourite thing
As the drops end and birds sing
And as it dries on earth below
Out comes a stunning rainbow

Holidays

Holidays can be so great
The family time can be first rate
Though these times can stir up rue
Because they are now without you

The gifts under the Christmas tree
Can be quite the sight to see
The bright colors against the green
One loves to have seen

The crackling fire and holiday baking
One sees memories in the making
Even with the people not there
There's still people who do care

With holiday season getting near
Full of good times and no fear
Hope it's great for one and all
Even without those who won't call

Society

It's not a crime to cry
To tell the truth and not a lie
Yet it does seems so rare
It's like no one would dare

Dare to resist all of society
Dare to not focus on propriety
To not conform but to stand out
To still have a voice against those with clout

Society tells and people believe
Yet they give nothing for us to receive
Though still one plays the part
And mesh together, not stand apart

And thus begins the downfall
Of people, not one but all
For few resist society's rules
Some toe it's line like mules

No judgement here however
For this has gone on since forever
But still I hope and pray
That society might change in some way

Safe Place

A warm crackling fireplace
With a basket of logs just in case
Two empty chairs facing it
Yet is not lonely, not a bit

For just a little further in
There's a family raising such a din
With kids laughing and adults talking
With pets running and teens walking

A home that is a safe place
With a smile on each face
One sees love in their eyes
With more joy on the rise

Perhaps it is a holiday season
Perhaps it doesn't need a reason
Perhaps just a family enjoying each other
Something that could last forever

A hug here and a kiss there
So much caring everywhere
Around a bright crackling fire
Where joy and love never tire

History

To the me that used to be
How I wish that you could see
I know you're living in the how
We became who we are now

Though the scars haven't healed yet
Though people have left that we met
And those who said they would stay
Turned their back and left anyway

We are getting stronger and tougher
Even as life keeps getting rougher
We rise every time we fall
And we have withstood it all

Though we might be getting colder
The more we grow and get older
It is harder to bring us to the ground
With this new armor we have found

Letter

Sitting down with a pen and pad
Talking about the good and the bad
Writing a letter to younger me
Hoping some day that I will see

The person that I will someday be
Someone who is loved and free
Learning to love myself even more
Trying to be truthful to the core

Remind myself that it gets better
As I continue on in this letter
Perhaps we'll reach our all time low
And happiness we'll never know

But the light does start to shine
And we stop faking being fine
And we'll hope that older me
Becomes the one we both want to be

Call

For as long as you're near
I will stay alive and here
Because I'd never want to hurt you
Or make you ever feel rue

I don't want to break your heart
Or ever seen you torn apart
I don't want you to ever hear
That I gave it all up to fear

Fear that it'll overwhelm me
Blind me to the point I can't see
Fear that my breath will slip away
Fear that I'll give up in every way

But I promise to stay here for you
I promise to breathe and live too
Even when I'm fighting I'll smile
Through every heart ache and trial

I'll build you up and watch your rise
And make sure tears don't fill your eyes
I'll stick beside you through it all
So that you never get that call

Alone

She sits alone in the dark
Hearing the tune of a meadowlark
Her hope begins to fade and leave
She prays to Him for some reprieve

In despair she stares up at the sky
As her eyes fill and she begins to cry
Because she lost all her self esteem
Finding out life's not as smooth as it may seem

Never knew people could break her heart
Into a thousand pieces, her life was torn apart
It was the people close to her that gave her pain
She tried to fight it or even to explain

When others told her to just cut them off
But she couldn't cause it would be too tough
She would do anything not to cause pain
Even if it meant loss and no gain

So she would continue to stare at the sky
Questioning why she should even try
Try to live but for what reason
Trying to survive this dark season

Music

There's beauty in the sound
The melody flows all around
It moves like the breeze
Crossing countries and seas

Moves people's mind and heart
And unites people torn apart
The tones carry you through
Making connections with all not a few

It's beauty flows on the page
When performed on stage
Through music or song
The story moves you along

Each note hitting a different chord
The tunes leave the audience floored
It connects people across the land
Meeting peoples music needs in demand

The One

Hopeful for tomorrow
A world void of sorrow
Where there are no more tears
A world without doubts and fears

In the depressing moments of today
Where you're scared and don't know what to say
When the darkness overwhelms you
Where your vision blurs and you have no view

View of what tomorrow could be
And all the wonders that one might see
Where you will never miss anyone
Where the battle's won and the war is done

When you'll be with one who knows it all
All because you didn't give in but answered the call
One who never leave you or forsake you
One who takes away all of your rue

Mind

Saying things you'd never say to anyone
Giving up and just wanting to be done
Tearing yourself down when you are low
Growing yourself so that you don't grow

Telling yourself you're not good enough
When people leave and times get tough
Feeling not enough to make people stay
That you stop trying for they'll leave anyway

Starving yourself and making yourself ill
To fight off the thoughts you wish you could kill
But still they rise up and overwhelm your mind
Doubts and worries of each and every kind

Fighting the urge to admit to defeat
Hiding from a version you never want to meet
A version much darker and in so much pain
Praying and hoping you'll pick a different lane

Watching you struggle just to survive
Waiting for the day that you will just thrive
That you will see beauty when you look in the
mirror
And be able to fight every doubt and fear

What If

What if I gave up tonight
What if I just threw the fight
What if I can't stop grieving
The pain of them leaving

While I know I shouldn't do it
Some days I just want to quit
Quit trying to just survive
And learning how to thrive

Maybe if I was to go
No one would ever know
The pain that I go through
And every day that's filled with rue

I won't give up on my life though
How much I fight you'll never know
I would never want to hurt anyone
Even if I myself am just so done

I'll live for my family and friends
No matter how each day ends
I'll keep breathing and living
And learn to care and start thriving

Forgiveness

Holding on to all this pain
Brings all loss and but not gain
Praying that someday I'll not cry
About the times that I truly did try

Trying to simply to forgive and forget
To not remember the new you I met
The memories keep flooding my mind
The scars from events of every kind

Yet holding on gives you control
And that is simply not your role
For you charged me many a tear
That I'm surprised I'm still here

As I try and learn to forgive you
I remember the undeserving rue
I didn't deserve the pain you gave
To the one who I wanted to save

But that version of me is lost
You may ask at what cost
The cost of letting go
A cost you will never truly know

Healing

Seems like it has been years of patience
Ages of following my conscience
Hoping someday it'll bring my healing
And make me have more feeling

It's as if my heart has turned to stone
From all the times I have felt alone
Having become as cold as ice
Due to being hurt more than once or twice

Being told that I should just move on
From the people who are simply gone
As if I can get over everything
Perhaps if it was just a fling

But family also decided to leave
Leave me alone to quietly grieve
In all this pain and suffering
Not truly caring about anything

Yet I still paint a smile on my face
I'll work hard to keep the same pace
Praying that one day I'll have feeling
And that that day will bring me healing

Fire

A fire burns fierce in my soul
Not just a part but the whole
Spurring me on to something
Something bigger than everything

Motivating me to change the fight
To change it for what is right
The right to live and not die
The right to not give up but try

Try to push for something great
To perhaps go against my fate
Fate that I created and destroyed
Proving that I will not by toyed

By those who seek my fall
Those who take not parts but all
All of my hope and my dreams
Tearing my life right at the seams

Today I'll light the fire in
Into my life for this fight to win
And give me the will to breathe and try
To fight for this life and refuse to die

Solo

Perhaps if you only knew
Just how much I missed you
When I was down so low
Saying things I hope you'll never know

Know what it's like to not believe
That it's not your fault when people leave
Even though you sometimes doubt it
Because they don't seem to care even one bit

When they leave and close the door
You're left alone crying on the floor
The pain overwhelms and floods you
With all of the memories you wish you never
knew

The pain of loving someone that much
And missing the feel of their touch
Now you've become stronger while solo
By ways that they'll never know

Hope

Not in this life do I find belief
In a world so full of grief
Hoping for something new
Praying for some sort of clue

That this is not for forever
That one day they'll be together
With those who truly care
Having a love that is becoming so rare

There's hope that some people hold
While my heart slowly turns cold
From this life that's hardened me
To the point that I can barely see

Instead of drowning in self pity
I focus on One who watches over me
Who carried me through the darkest days
Who guides me in al of the ways

Who helps me to believe in me
So that perhaps one day I'll see
The person that He's always seen
Someone who is beautifully washed clean

www.ingramcontent.com/pod-product-compliance
Lightning Source LLC
Chambersburg PA
CBHW051720130826
49812CB00034B/1269
9789357212076